INSPIRED

CHURCHES OF SEATTLE

Rick Grant

photography by Lara Swimmer

Documentary Media

Seattle, Washington

INSPIRED
CHURCHES OF SEATTLE

© 2013 Rick Grant

All rights reserved. No part of this book may be reproduced or utilized in any form without the prior written consent of the publisher.

First Edition
Printed in Canada

Author: Rick Grant
Produced by Documentary Media, Seattle, Washington
Book Design: Paul Langland Design
Photography: Lara Swimmer

Library of Congress Cataloging-in-Publication Data
Grant, Rick, 1956-
Inspired : churches of Seattle / Rick Grant ; photography by Lara Swimmer. — 1st ed.
　pages cm
Includes bibliographical references.
ISBN 978-1-933245-31-7
1. Christianity—Washington (State)—Seattle. 2. Seattle (Wash.)—Church history. 3. Church buildings—Washington (State)—Seattle. I. Title.
BR560.S45G73 2013
280.09797'772—dc23
2013020482

Images
Page 2: Saint Mark's Cathedral
Page 5: St. Paul's
Page 6: Chapel of Saint Ignatius
Page 160: Chapel of Saint Ignatius

For further information about this book or its content contact Rick Grant at ricgrant1@gmail.com or www.inspired-seattle.com

Table of Contents

Introduction	8		
History	12		

First Hill — 22

Chapel of Saint Ignatius	24
Immaculate Conception Church	26
Mount Zion Baptist Church	28
St. James Cathedral	30
Seattle First Baptist Church	34
Seattle First Presbyterian Church	36
Trinity Parish Church	38

Downtown — 40

First Church – First United Methodist Church of Seattle — 42
Gethsemane Lutheran Church — 44
Immanuel Lutheran — 48
Plymouth Church – United Church of Christ — 50
Saint Spiridon Orthodox Cathedral — 52

Capitol Hill — 54

Epiphany of Seattle — 56
First A.M.E. Church – Seattle — 58
Greek Orthodox Church of the Assumption — 60
Holy Names Academy Chapel — 62
St. Demetrios Greek Orthodox Church — 64
St. Joseph — 66
Saint Mark's Cathedral — 68
St. Patrick — 72
Saint Nicholas Russian Orthodox Cathedral — 74

University District — 76

Blessed Sacrament Church — 78
University Christian Church — 82
University Congregational Church — 84
University Presbyterian Church — 86
University Unitarian Church — 88
Seattle Vineyard — 90

Eastside — 92

Bellevue Presbyterian Church — 94
Christ Church Kirkland — 96
Eastridge Church — 98
Mars Hill Church Bellevue — 100
Mary Queen of Peace — 104
Mercer Island Presbyterian Church — 106
Overlake Christian Church — 108

Queen Anne — 110

Bethany Presbyterian Church — 112
First Free Methodist Church — 114
Queen Anne Baptist Church — 116
Queen Anne Lutheran Church — 118
Sacred Heart of Jesus — 120
St. Paul's Episcopal Church — 122
Seattle Church of Christ — 126

Southwest — 128

Fauntleroy Church – United Church of Christ — 130
Holy Rosary — 132
Japanese Baptist Church — 134
Our Lady of Mount Virgin — 136
St. Edward — 138

Northwest — 142

Bethany Community Church — 144
Calvary Christian Assembly — 148
Green Lake United Methodist Church — 150
Interfaith Community Sanctuary — 152
Our Lady of Fatima — 154
Phinney Ridge Lutheran Church — 156

Acknowledgments — 158
Bibliography — 159

Introduction

Chapel of Saint Ignatius

Let's start with the Big Question: Are there more churches in Seattle or Starbucks?

Starbucks? Makes sense. When you think of Seattle, you think of Starbucks and the coffee culture it spawned, where the worship of java has been taken to a spiritual level. In fact, Starbucks in Seattle seems to possess the 3 Omni's that theologians have historically attributed to God—omnipotence (unlimited influence), omniscience (overseeing everything), and of course, omnipresence.

Contrast this with how churches in Seattle are often seen. Relative to other areas of the country, we in Seattle and the Northwest are considered the unchurched, the Nones (not nuns), the latter referring to the fact that more people claim none when asked about religious identification than in any other section of the United States. Spirituality in Seattle is considered cool enough, but when it comes to church attendance/membership or other indicators of church commitment, we appear skittish.

On top of this, we in Seattle experience what might be called the irony of topography. With the city dwarfed by the towering presence of the Olympics and the Cascades, we somehow feel a sense of awe and respect for the grandeur of our surroundings but aren't sure whether to attribute it to nature or nature's God or to what exactly.

So is Seattle really God's Country that isn't? An ecclesiastical wasteland embracing only some kind of secular spirituality? Hardly. Churches are a dynamic part of the current and historical culture of Seattle, affecting and contributing to all elements of the society. Ye of little faith should check out the following:

■ There are more than 400 churches in the Seattle area (the numbers fluctuate at times), competing with the 471 Starbucks stores.

■ Every weekend tens of thousands of Seattleites make a mass migration to some kind of worship service.

- Seattle churches have often been among the largest of their denomination in the country; for many years in the early 20th century, Seattle's First Presbyterian Church had the largest membership of any Presbyterian church in the country or the world.
- Several Seattle churches have won awards for architecture and are considered some of the most beautiful and ornate in the country.
- We've had a saint in our midst. St. Frances Xavier Cabrini, the first American to be canonized, lived in Seattle from 1903 to 1916.

Gethsemane Lutheran Church

More than considering saints and statistics, churches are part of our everyday Seattle experience. Whether glimpsing the majestic Saint Mark's from I-5, viewing the litany of historic churches on First Hill, or just walking through the University District or Queen Anne, we see the spires and steeples and sense the tradition. Some of us attend services, some of us volunteer through church organizations, some of us send our kids to religious schools, and many of us use church facilities to get married or buried.

Talking about the impact of religion in the Pacific Northwest in their book *Roots and Branches,* Junius Rochester and David M. Buerge wrote: "American immigration into the Pacific Northwest began as a religious crusade; much of Washington's health, educational, and welfare establishment owes its existence and character to religious groups, and some of its politics turned on issues generated from within religious organizations." This certainly is true in Seattle, especially in the area of social outreach, where everything from hospitals to homeless shelters to food banks often find their genesis and upkeep with church folk.

But talking about the effect and influence doesn't imply a homogeneity of belief or practice among the churches of Seattle. At last count there were more than 100 different denominations represented in the area from all sides of the theological spectrum. Patricia O'Connell Killen in her book *Religion and Public Life in the Pacific Northwest: The None Zone* talked about the "religious environment where boundaries and identities are fluid," with a "highly elastic religious reality." Seattleites aren't ones to be pigeonholed in any area of their lives.

What church people in Seattle have in common are their stories. To know Seattle's churches is to know stories of people, stories of buildings, stories of disputes and scandals, and stories of persistent love. To tell these stories we will start with the history of churches in the area, giving some background on the communities of faith and who did what when. Then we will showcase individual churches in specific neighborhoods and see what makes them special.

With hundreds of churches in the Seattle area, we unfortunately couldn't include all and so chose 52 based on considerations such as architecture, historical background, and a desire for denominational diversity. We understand that many beautiful and dynamic churches (and temples, mosques, etc.) were left out and hope these many will be showcased in follow-ups to this book.

So enjoy. We hope that, like a good cup of coffee, this book on the architecture and heritage of Seattle's churches will both warm you and get you pumped about an indispensable aspect of Seattle's rich culture.

Interfaith Community Sanctuary

History

Church of the Sacred Heart of Jesus, Sixth Avenue and Bell Street. University of Washington Libraries, Special Collections, A. Curtis 01252

"Charity, my friends, charity."

As itinerant Catholic priest Father Modeste Demers invoked this phrase to a ragtag assemblage of sinners and saints in the cookhouse of Henry Yesler's lumber mill in 1853, we are left to wonder what inspired this homiletic choice. Perhaps the good father (who had just canoed into the area) discovered he was preaching the first sermon in backwater Seattle and wanted the universal theme of love (charity) to become a self-fulfilling prophecy. Or perhaps Father Demers tapped into a prophecy of another sort, a foretelling of how this small group's coming together on the subject of charity would be a theme of Seattle's churches in the years to come.

Missionaries had started flocking to the Northwest in the 1830s, responding to a call among the various denominations to spread the gospel to the natives in the area. As an outpost or town (say Walla Walla or Vancouver) became established, ministers would follow, hoping to establish a church and sometimes social services in these pre-territorial areas. After the native evangelism met with some hostilities (missionaries Dr. Marcus Whitman and his wife, Narcissa, were killed in 1847) and lackluster results, the focus became more on ministry to the influx of white settlers.

The first minister stationed in Seattle was Reverend David E. Blaine. He and his wife, Catharine (Seattle's first schoolteacher), came west as missionaries in the early 1850s.

They built Seattle's first church, the Methodist Episcopal Church, in 1855 on two lots on the corner of Second and Columbia. This house of worship became known as the "White Church," which Seattle historian Junius Rochester wryly noted later became a saloon, restaurant, and vaudeville house with subsequent ownerships.

Soon other denominations wanted to join the fun. Reverend Daniel Bagley, the "Father of the University of Washington," established Seattle's second church (the Brown Church) in 1865 for the Methodist Protestants. This was followed in successive years by the Plymouth Congregational Church, First Baptist Church, First Presbyterian Church, Gethsemane Lutheran, and Trinity Church, an Episcopal Church that boasted the first pipe organ in Washington Territory. Toward the end of the century the First Church of Christ, Scientist, was established, along with African Methodist Episcopal (AME) and the first Jewish congregation, Bikur Cholim Machzikay Hadath.

Following Father Demers's lead, the robust Father Francis Xavier Prefontaine came into Seattle's picture in 1867, when only 10 of the area's 600 citizens were reportedly Roman Catholic. After renting a house on Third Avenue and saying his first mass to a congregation of two women (who hopefully prayed loudly), the pragmatic priest set about building Our Lady of Good Help, dedicated in the fall of 1870. By 1883 the church was boasting a congregation of 600.

The growth of these new churches paralleled the growth of the city, which in 1880 numbered only about 3,500 residents but grew to over 237,000 by 1910. This period was both dynamic and turbulent: dynamic because of an economic boom (the connection of the railroads to Seattle, industries such as fishing and shipbuilding, the 1897 discovery of gold in the Klondike), turbulent because the growth was tempered by the devastating fire of 1889 and the nationwide depression of 1893. The churches ministered to the growing population during the ebbs and flows, with church people involved in the establishment of schools and social services and reaching out to the groups of African-Americans, Japanese, Chinese, Italians, and Scandinavians coming into the area.

Seattle's first church, First Methodist Episcopal, was built along with a parsonage in 1855 at Second and Columbia. Museum of History & Industry

Mark Matthews: Dynamic Pastor

In 1902 a whirlwind from Georgia descended on the First Presbyterian Church of Seattle. His name was Mark Matthews, and his 38-year ministry was a dynamic combination of preaching and living the social gospel. As Whitworth professor Dale Soden wrote in his biography of Matthews: "No other clergyman wielded greater influence either socially or politically in the Pacific Northwest during the first half of the twentieth century."

The six-foot-five, reed-thin Matthews could fire and brimstone with the best of them, using hair-curling invective against both lazy Christians and corrupt politicians. A strong advocate of Progressive reforms and the "social gospel," Matthews wanted to make Seattle a righteous community through addressing its ills (drinking, prostitution, gambling) and meeting its needs (with an abundance of community work at hospitals, orphanages, libraries, day nurseries, and an unemployment bureau). He immersed himself in the political controversies of the day, and famously feuded with Mayor Hiram Gill, whom he had secretly investigated for corruption.

During his tenure at First Pres, the church boasted the largest Presbyterian membership in the world. A bust of Matthews in Denny Park is the only such public tribute to a minister in Seattle, where the words are inscribed: "Preacher of the Word of God and Friend to Man."

The Reverend Mark A. Matthews, Southern-born supporter of the Social Gospel movement, became the outspoken pastor of Seattle's First Presbyterian Church in 1902. Museum of History & Industry

This upswing in church attendance from the late 1880s to World War I was accompanied by the largest congregational growth in Seattle's history. Brand-new churches were erected; older churches ran out of room and built new and bigger establishments. In 1907 alone there were 20 new church buildings erected, for the then-whopping sum of $1,500,000.

Seattle as a church town? In his book *History of Seattle*, published in 1916, author Clarence Bagley (son of Daniel) wrote, "The city's people have always been church-goers. Some of the largest congregations in the world are to be found in Seattle; and in a score of years they have extended their work until every section of the city where there is a growing community has its church or chapel or mission."

Street of dreams, Seattle 1890. Shown from left are First Presbyterian Church, the Martin Van Buren Stacy home, and the First Methodist-Episcopal Church on Third Avenue. University of Washington Libraries, Special Collections, Warner 191x

Some at the time may have begged to differ with Bagley's churchgoer tag, but there was no doubt that churches were growing and following the people to their new neighborhoods.

With this growth, those shepherding these flocks became well known themselves, leading their congregations and becoming community pillars. The charismatic Reverend Mark Matthews (see sidebar), the only Seattle minister with his own public statue (Denny Park), took First Presbyterian Church from 400 members and being in debt in 1901 to 5,240 members in 1909, the largest Presbyterian enrollment in the country. In 1903, Dr. Hans Andreas Stub took over at Immanuel Lutheran and stayed pastor until 1957, marrying a massive 3,000+ couples during that period! Father Edward John O'Dea led what became the Diocese of Seattle for 36 years (1896-1932), as the Roman Catholic population grew exponentially and built many churches, hospitals, and schools.

Indeed much was done during this period for the city's "poor and needy," in line with the concurrent "Social Gospel" movement. The rapid growth of the population put stresses on urban areas, and the churches strove to be in the forefront with various "works of mercy." The Sisters of Providence organized Providence Hospital, the Episcopal Church built Grace Hospital, the Methodists established a Deaconess Home, and Kenney Presbyterian Home as well as other homes for the elderly were established, along with several orphanages.

After World War I the Seattle churches, like those throughout the country, addressed issues that both unified and polarized them. As to the former, years of lobbying and influence among the ministers and laity helped lead to Prohibition in 1919 and the passing of the 19th Amendment in 1920, allowing women to vote. Also in 1919 the Seattle Federation of Churches was organized, with 62 congregations coming together to pursue common goals and cooperative work.

But churches also became polarized over how to deal with their rapidly changing world. Darwin's theory of evolution, brought into the national consciousness with the Scopes Monkey Trial of 1925, challenged the Christian worldview of many. The authority of Scripture was also being challenged, with modern methods of historical criticism being used on the texts. Some liberals embraced the new ways of thinking and tried to adjust the gospel to the changes; conservatives blanched at the new secular "modernism" and emphasized the fundamentals of faith.

And then there were the Communists. Saint Spiridon Orthodox Cathedral, founded in Seattle in 1895, was actually grabbed by court order when the Communists in Russia gained control, a procedure the new Soviet Union tried with several Orthodox churches in the United States. When hearing of this attempt, angry parishioners removed religious articles at night and set up services in a nearby church. Nipping this takeover in the bud, an independent St. Spiridon later set up shop at its current location on Yale Avenue.

As the Great Depression hit Seattle in the 1930s, the churches were more than just depressed that Prohibition had been

GERTRUDE APEL: FOREMOTHER OF FAITH

From her early childhood on a farm in central Minnesota, Gertrude Louise Apel (1896-1966) knew she wanted to be a Methodist minister. She also knew the challenges involved in that quest: church women in the early 20th century more often cleaned the pulpit than preached from it. Undaunted, Gertrude paved her own path by attending seminary in Chicago, working as a missionary, and doing some circuit-riding preaching in Washington's Methow Valley.

But it was in Seattle that Dr. Apel's dreams came to fruition. She became Christian education director and associate pastor of the new Trinity Methodist Church in northwest Seattle (1929-1930), worked for 28 years as leader and then general secretary of what later became known as the Church Council of Greater Seattle, and in her last years became founding pastor of the Marine View Methodist Church in Federal Way (1959-1966). Her ecumenical efforts with the Council of Churches were especially noteworthy, as she used her leadership skills to wade through the inevitable controversies and work toward church unity, peace, and religious education.

Those who knew Dr. Apel praise both her creative personality and abundance of abilities, describing her as a Jill of all trades who enjoyed music, art, hiking, fishing, woodcraft, and even electrical work. By the time of her death she had cemented her place as a nationally recognized church leader and role model for other women wanting to minister.

repealed. In their excellent book *Roots and Branches* about the religious history of Washington State, authors David Buerge and Junius Rochester lamented that during this period "congregations sank, clerics' salaries were slashed, programs were cut back or eliminated, and some churches were closed and abandoned." Along with the cutbacks and closures was a quandary about what to do: some ministries gave handouts,

Dr. Gertrude Apel.
Museum of History & Industry

The Ecumenical "Challenge"

With a strong history of ecumenical cooperation but an acknowledgment of polarization over the spiritual and secular issues of the day, Seattle seemed ripe for a public discourse on religious beliefs and their effect on the community and its people. This came to fruition in 1960 with the television show *Challenge*, which featured a rabbi, a Catholic priest, and a Protestant minister and became a popular and award-winning show that lasted until the mid 1970s.

The show idea was originally broached in the early 1950s by Rabbi Raphael Levine of Temple De Hirsch but didn't materialize until 1960, when political issues around the presidential election sparked the type of controversy an inter-religious dialogue could shine a light on. KOMO TV embraced the idea, and in September 1960, "Can We Have a Catholic President?" was aired, featuring Father William Treacy, Rabbi Raphael Levine, and the Reverend Martin Goslin of Plymouth Congregational Church.

Discussing the show in *Roots and Branches*, the authors wrote that seeing "representatives of faiths that share a long and bitter history of antagonism discussing the issues dividing them in a lively, rational, and amiable manner was extraordinary." The quality and reconciliatory attitude of the show, along with its popular appeal, was a highlight in the religious history of Seattle.

KOMO TV commentators and Brotherhood Week cochairmen, from left: University Methodist Church Reverend Dr. Lynn H. Corson, St. Patrick's Church administrator Father William Treacy, and Temple De Hirsch Rabbi Raphael Levine

some ministers like the fiery Reverend Fred Shorter called for more radical "Socialistic" solutions from his newly established Church of the People in the University District. History doesn't say if the Communists contacted Reverend Shorter after striking out at Saint Spiridon.

Other issues evolved when the Japanese attacked Pearl Harbor in 1941 and Japanese-Americans in the area were sent to relocation and internment camps. The Japanese had come to Seattle before the turn of the century to work in the railroads, sawmills, and canneries and had maintained a significant influence in the area (the Seattle Japanese Baptist Church was organized in 1899). Although several preachers in the area seemed apathetic about the relocation, others vehemently opposed it, with several churches' members going to Tacoma to protest the loading of Japanese-Americans onto trains to the camps.

The baby boom population growth after World War II led to a strong upsurge in church membership and the building of new churches in the suburbs (especially the Eastside). With the new contemporary church buildings came new leadership; it was in 1958 that the much-respected

Reverend Dale Turner started his 24-year run as senior minister of the University Congregational Church in the University District. The Church Council of Greater Seattle (formerly the Seattle Federation of Churches) was very active during these and subsequent years.

During this period a Norwegian-born Methodist clergyman named Abraham Vereide was making his mark both locally and nationally. Moving to Seattle in 1916, Vereide and his wife, Mattie, were an integral part of social-justice ministries in the city, with Abraham becoming the founder of Goodwill Industries of Seattle. From his base here Vereide founded the prayer breakfast movement in the United States in 1935, and in 1953 started the Presidential Prayer Breakfast, currently called the National Prayer Breakfast, with over 3,500 invitees from 100 countries.

With the dawn of the 1960s Seattle focused on its upcoming World's Fair, and the churches and Christian agencies in the area responded by sponsoring a Christian Pavilion adjacent to the U.S. Science Pavilion. Visited by close to a million people during the six-month fair, the Christian Pavilion featured a meditation chapel, a small theater, and two pieces of artwork produced for the occasion: a stained glass window and a wood mosaic panel of Christ and the children.

As the '60s progressed, several Seattle churches became involved in the civil rights movement. At the forefront of this movement was the Reverend John Adams, who held the pastorate at First African Methodist Episcopal Church from 1962 to 1968. During this period Adams chaired the Central Area Civil Rights Committee and was a cofounder of the country's first war-on-poverty agency, the Central Area Motivation Program (CAMP).

Along with civil rights, the issues during the 1960s and 1970s that challenged the country (the war in Vietnam, the feminist movement) also polarized Seattle's liberal and conservative churches, but there were attempts to work together on the issues as well. A program titled CURE (Churches United for Racial Equality)

Top: The Christian Pavilion at the 1962 Seattle World's Fair. The mural shown was a mosaic comprised of 4,385 pieces of colored glass. Photography by Max Jensen provided courtesy of the Seattle Public Library and the Seattle Center Foundation
Below: Rev. Samuel McKinney, pastor of Seattle's Mount Zion Baptist Church from 1958 to 1998, was a major force in the community during his years of leadership. Post-Intelligencer *Collection, Museum of History & Industry*

Opposite: First Methodist Episcopal Church, 1952—now a Mars Hill Church. University of Washington Libraries, Special Collections, DM 1639
Below: Christ the King Lutheran Church was built in Bellevue in 1956. University of Washington Libraries, Special Collections, Todd 25022a

helped pass an open-housing ordinance, and the Greater Seattle Council of Churches worked to eliminate discrimination in public facilities. The television program *Challenge* (see sidebar), running from 1960 to the mid 1970s, showcased a rabbi (Raphael Levine of Temple De Hirsch), a priest (Father William Treacy), and various Protestant ministers (culled from several denominations) discussing issues of the day.

In the 1980s the Moral Majority emerged as a political and spiritual force nationally, but the movements in the Seattle churches tended more toward recognizing the rights of individuals and disenfranchised groups. Acceptance of women, gays and lesbians, and transgendered people became rallying points in the Roman Catholic, Episcopal, and other mainline denominations in the area, a movement that continues to this day. And over these years various Hispanic congregations cropped up throughout the city.

In 1996, WSU graduate Mark Driscoll and his wife, Grace, started a Bible study in their Seattle home that soon became Mars Hill Church, considered at the cutting edge of the nationwide "emergent church" movement. Coming from a Reformed Christian tradition, the church grew rapidly and moved into a renovated hardware store in Ballard in 2003. Since then the ministry has reached megachurch status, with 14 church campuses spread out over four states.

With the advent of the 21st century, churches are still a major presence in Seattle and continue to affect its culture and institutions. Although Seattle and the Northwest are still considered relatively "unchurched" vis-à-vis the rest of the country, the vibrant tradition of immigrant outreach, ecumenicalism, and acts of mercy goes unabated and is a central factor in the continuing health of the city.

It seems that Father Demers truly was a prophet.

Chapel of Saint Ignatius

First Hill

Chapel of Saint Ignatius

If you're looking for a sacred space with a unique modern design and a meditative ambience, you should make it a point to visit the Chapel of Saint Ignatius, on the Seattle University campus. Designed by locally born New York architect Steven Holl in 1997, the chapel won a design award from the New York chapter of the American Institute of Architects.

The chapel is named after St. Ignatius Loyola, founder of the Jesuit order, which runs Seattle University. The chapel's concept reflects St. Ignatius's take on the spiritual life, composed of lights and darknesses he called "consolations and desolation" in his famous book *The Spiritual Exercises of St. Ignatius of Loyola*.

For more information please refer to *The Chapel of St. Ignatius*, a coffee-table book published in 1999 showcasing the principles and motivations behind the design and construction of the church.

Architecture:
Steven Holl, 1997

Immaculate Conception Church

Perched on the top of First Hill is Immaculate Conception Church, whose members see themselves as a congregation "placed in the heart of the community to be the heart of the community." This mission not only is current but also has been fulfilled throughout the years, as Immaculate Conception is the oldest standing Catholic church in Seattle and one of the most influential.

The church was declared a city landmark in 1977, and for many good reasons. It features a grotto (a small but exact replica of the Lourdes grotto in France), hand-painted frescoes from the 1920s, statues dating from 1890 to the 1920s, and beautiful stained glass windows. The church is closely connected to Seattle University; SU stands on the site of the first Immaculate Conception church building, and the student body still congregates there for larger group gatherings.

Of the many ministries of the church, music is often showcased, offering everything from traditional old-world style to contemporary to gospel. The Immaculate Conception Church Change Team has recently focused on helping members develop healthy lifestyles.

Architecture:
Williams and Clark, 1904

Mount Zion Baptist Church

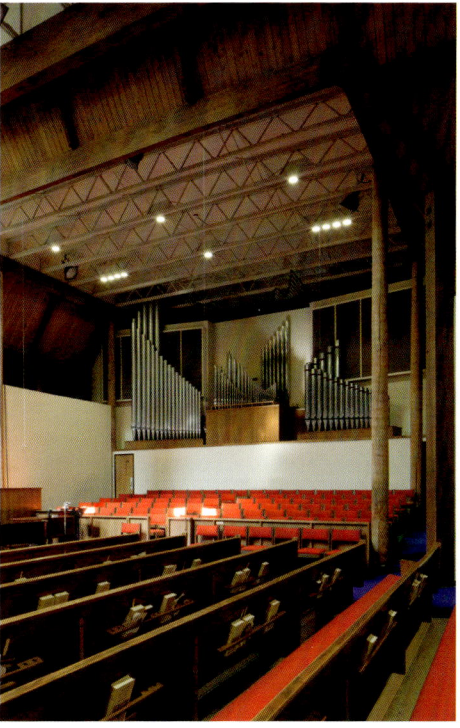

One of Seattle's most influential churches is Mount Zion Baptist, a beacon of spiritual insight and social and political activism for over a century.

After a small group of African-Americans held prayer services in their homes in 1890, the momentum for a church started to build and the Mount Zion Baptist Church was established. The first church structure was built in 1920 at the corner of 19th and East Madison. The congregation continued to grow, making it necessary to replace the building with a new one, which opened for worship in October 1975 and has been updated over the years. Visitors will find remnants of the original church throughout.

Mount Zion Baptist Church is known throughout the region and the country for the inspiring preaching and its music ministry. The church has a variety of other noteworthy programs, including a Christian Education Department, a mentoring program, and a Christian Arts Ministry that includes dance and drama.

Architecture:
Durham, Anderson, and Freed, 1975

St. James Cathedral

One of Seattle's most famous and recognizable churches is St. James Cathedral, whose soaring 167-foot twin towers are a mainstay of the First Hill skyline. Beyond the striking Italian Renaissance architecture, the church is known for its beautiful liturgies and outreach to the poor, and is the cathedral church for the Catholic Archdiocese of Seattle.

A few years after the cathedral's dedication in 1907, its great dome collapsed during a heavy snowstorm in 1916, and the church was closed for more than a year for repairs. Declared a city landmark in 1984, the church has been through a series of renovations, the last being in 1994. As part of this latest renovation, the relics of St. Frances Xavier Cabrini, who had attended the church when she worked in Seattle from 1903 to 1916, were sealed beneath the altar.

The church contains a treasure trove of artistic wonders, including ceremonial bronze doors and tabernacle by German sculptor Ulrich Henn, an award-winning Shrine of the Blessed Virgin Mary, and the Cathedral Chapel containing the 15th-century painting *Madonna and Child with Saints* by Neri di Bicci. Throughout the church is a large collection of stained glass windows by

renowned artists Charles Connick and Hans Gottfried von Stockhausen. The church also cultivates the arts with its members and the community and has a highly acclaimed music program.

Architecture:
Heins & LaFarge, 1907
Bumgardner Architects, 1994
Susan Jones Architect, 1994
    (Marian Chapel)

"Truly I tell you, whatever you did for one of the least of these brothers and sisters of mine, you did for me."

Jesus Christ

Seattle First Baptist Church

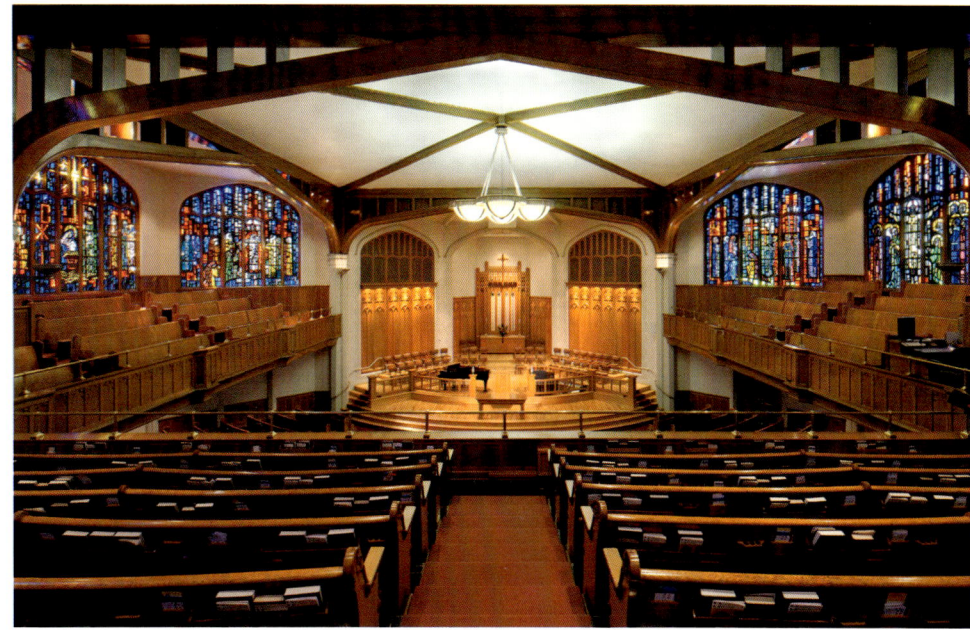

A can't-miss landmark on First Hill, Seattle First Baptist Church was founded in 1869 and moved to its present location at the corner of Harvard and Seneca in September of 1912. With a ministry focused on "liberating the heart, engaging the mind, and embracing the world," Seattle First Baptist not only has deep roots historically in the Seattle area but also offers a creative set of programs and outreach alternatives.

The current sanctuary was designed in the English Medieval Gothic style with a spire and a presence that can be appreciated as far away as downtown and Capitol Hill. Inside is a beautiful array of stained glass windows depicting Old Testament stories and the life of Christ; along with the sanctuary there is the Hintz Memorial Chapel and a spacious Fellowship Hall. In 1981 the Sanctuary building of the church was declared a Seattle landmark.

The church embraces a progressive side of the Baptist faith and emphasizes its position as a welcoming and nurturing community. Its impressive programs include a Jazz Vespers group and a Diverse Harmony Choir.

Architecture:
U. Fay Grant, 1912

Seattle First Presbyterian Church

From its humble beginning in 1869, with a pastor transported by wagon train and canoe preaching to seven attendees, Seattle First Presbyterian has grown into one of Seattle's largest and most influential churches, with one of its most beautiful sanctuaries.

While the Reverend Mark Matthews pastored the church from 1902 to 1940, SFPC grew to 8,000 members and became the largest Presbyterian church in the world. A pattern of ministry surfaced at that time and has continued to this day in the areas of shaping public policy and care for society's poor and outcast (the church founded Harborview Hospital and Union Gospel Mission, both of which are still in operation).

Within the church the leadership promotes a course of "Mission, Vision, and Values," and seeks to connect its members to their spiritual gifts and talents. Its many programs include the arts and Mission and Outreach.

Architecture:
Gudmund Berge, 1962

Trinity Parish Church

Trinity Parish Church (Episcopal) is an open and affirming urban parish with a legacy of ministry reaching back almost 150 years. Established in 1865, Trinity became the mother church to later Episcopal outreaches in Seattle.

After the Great Fire of 1889 destroyed the original building at Third and Jefferson, Trinity was rebuilt in 1892 at Eighth and James in an English Gothic Revival design created by Henry F. Starbuck of Chicago. When another fire destroyed the interior of that building in 1902, local architect John Graham Sr. incorporated the still-standing exterior masonry of Wilkeson sandstone while expanding the transept and adding a bell tower and spire. This structure, finished in 1902 with German stained glass and an altar of Italian Carrara marble, is listed on the National Register of Historic Places and is a City of Seattle landmark. The Nisqually Earthquake on Ash Wednesday of 2001 caused significant damage, but after restoration and retrofitting, the church was reconsecrated on February 11, 2006.

Trinity is Seattle's oldest church structure and serves as the home of Northwest Harvest and its Cherry Street Food Bank.

Architecture:
Henry F. Starbuck, 1892

Plymouth Church

Downtown

First Church – First United Methodist Church of Seattle

You've heard the term "best of both worlds"? First United Methodist Church encapsulates that phrase, incorporating both the wisdom and tradition of being Seattle's oldest congregation while also embracing the contemporary outreach that inhabiting one of Seattle's newest sanctuaries represents.

As was discussed in the previous History chapter, soon after Reverend David Blaine and his new wife, Catharine, landed at Alki Point, they started a church at the corner of Second and Columbia. The church continued to grow in membership and influence, founding Seattle's General Hospital and a mission school and hosting a radio ministry for many years. The current building, on the corner of 2nd Avenue and Denny Way, was dedicated in 2010.

The mission of the church is "Love. Grow. Serve." The latter is put into practice with their Blaine Center (a 60-bed shelter for homeless men) and weekly shared breakfast that feeds as many as 500 people. Their creative ministry programs include Pax Christi Yoga, which combines the practice of yoga with a focus on Christian Scriptures.

Architecture:
Bassetti Architects, 2010

Gethsemane Lutheran Church

Gethsemane Lutheran is a captivating downtown church combining more than a century of progressive ministry with a beautiful new renovation, the Kindred Center. This Center includes an update of their 56-year-old sanctuary and exquisite jewel box chapel with an attached outdoor garden (think Garden of Gethsemane) meant to welcome the public into a quiet worship and meditation space.

Gethsemane Lutheran is the oldest Lutheran congregation in Seattle, founded in 1885. Bursting at the seams after a few years of ministry, the congregation decided to move in 1901 to its present site at the corner of Ninth and Stewart. The church is currently a member of the Evangelical Lutheran Church in America (ELCA).

The church outreach programs include the Compass Housing Alliance Center and the Hope Center, the base for Gethsemane Community Services. The church emphasizes inclusiveness and a focus on the liturgy in worship.

Architecture:
Paul Fritts and Company, 1956

"We are put on earth
for a little space that we might bear
the beams of love."

William Blake

Immanuel Lutheran

Immanuel means "God with us," and from every indication the Almighty has blessed Immanuel Lutheran with a long history of ministry and energetic outreach to the downtown/South Lake Union area.

Immanuel Lutheran was first organized in 1890 by a group of 33 Norwegian immigrants and pioneers. When Dr. and Mrs. H. A. Stub were called to the church in 1903, they began a 54-year pastorate at Immanuel, one of the longest in the history of the Pacific Northwest. The current church was built in 1912, and in the upcoming century Immanuel became one of the largest congregations in the West.

With their outreach Immanuel has established Immanuel Community Services, its own nonprofit, which includes a Food Bank, a Community Lunch, and a Recovery program. The church has a visual arts team and a music program described as "sometimes toe-stomping, and sometimes contemplative."

Architecture:
Watson W. Vernon, 1907

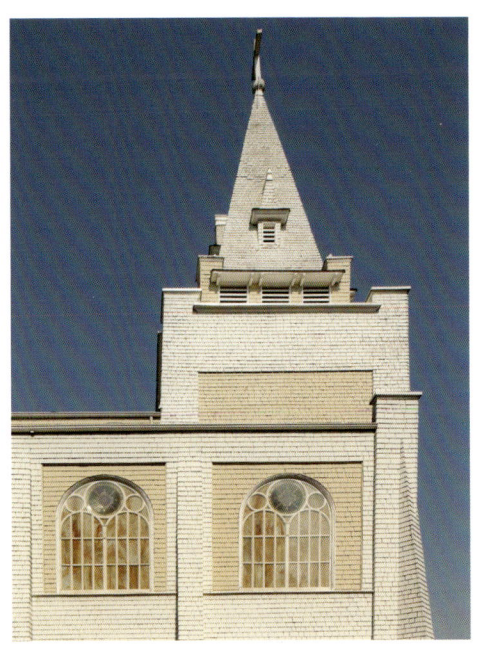

Plymouth Church – United Church of Christ

Plymouth Church, with its distinctive modern architecture and status as one of the oldest Protestant congregations in Seattle, is also one of Seattle's most renowned churches. In its more than 140 years of ministry, Plymouth has been committed to social justice and has helped spawn other Congregational churches in the area.

The first services of the church were held in 1869 in Yesler's Hall (a room above a drugstore in Pioneer Square), and over the years the congregation built three different churches. Plymouth's current home, built in 1967, has become a downtown landmark with its white coloring and oval-shaped design.

In 1960, Plymouth joined the United Church of Christ, a denomination currently of 5,000 churches and 1.2 million members dedicated to "Changing Lives, Extravagant Welcome, and Continuing Testament." Plymouth continues to be a voice of progressive theology in the Northwest and works for justice in the areas of homelessness, mental illness, immigrant issues, environmental justice, and GLBTQ rights.

Architecture:
Perry B. Johanson, 1967

Saint Spiridon Orthodox Cathedral

A jewel of a church in the South Lake Union area of downtown is Saint Spiridon Orthodox Cathedral, with its long history of ministry and distinctive architecture. The church celebrates its multi-ethnic diversity and Slavic Orthodox heritage and contains many beautiful historic icons.

Saint Spiridon was founded in 1895 by immigrants from Russia, Greece, and Eastern Europe. The Russian Revolution played a large role in the history of the church as several of the Russians who settled in Seattle after leaving the homeland began attending. Although current membership includes a large constituency of children and grandchildren of those who immigrated to Seattle, there is a conscious policy of welcoming newcomers.

Saint Spiridon is a member of the Orthodox Church in America, which has over 700 parishes and institutions throughout the United States, Canada, and Mexico. The denomination began in 1794, when eight Orthodox missionaries started an outreach to the native Alaskan population; Saint Spiridon sees itself as a direct descendant of this Russian Orthodox mission to Alaska.

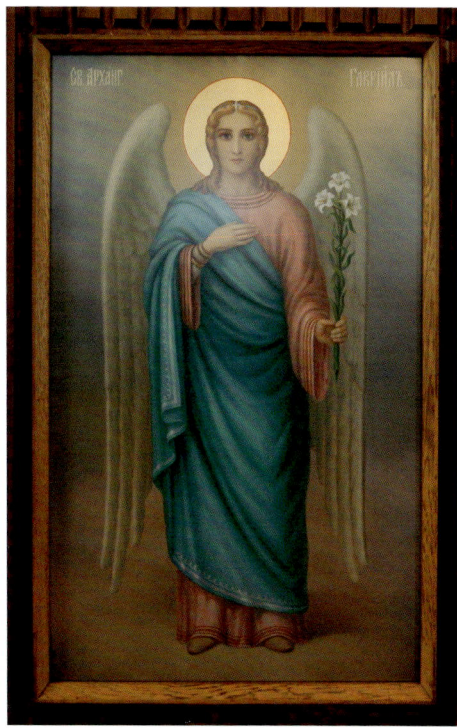

Architecture:
Ivan Palmaw, 1938

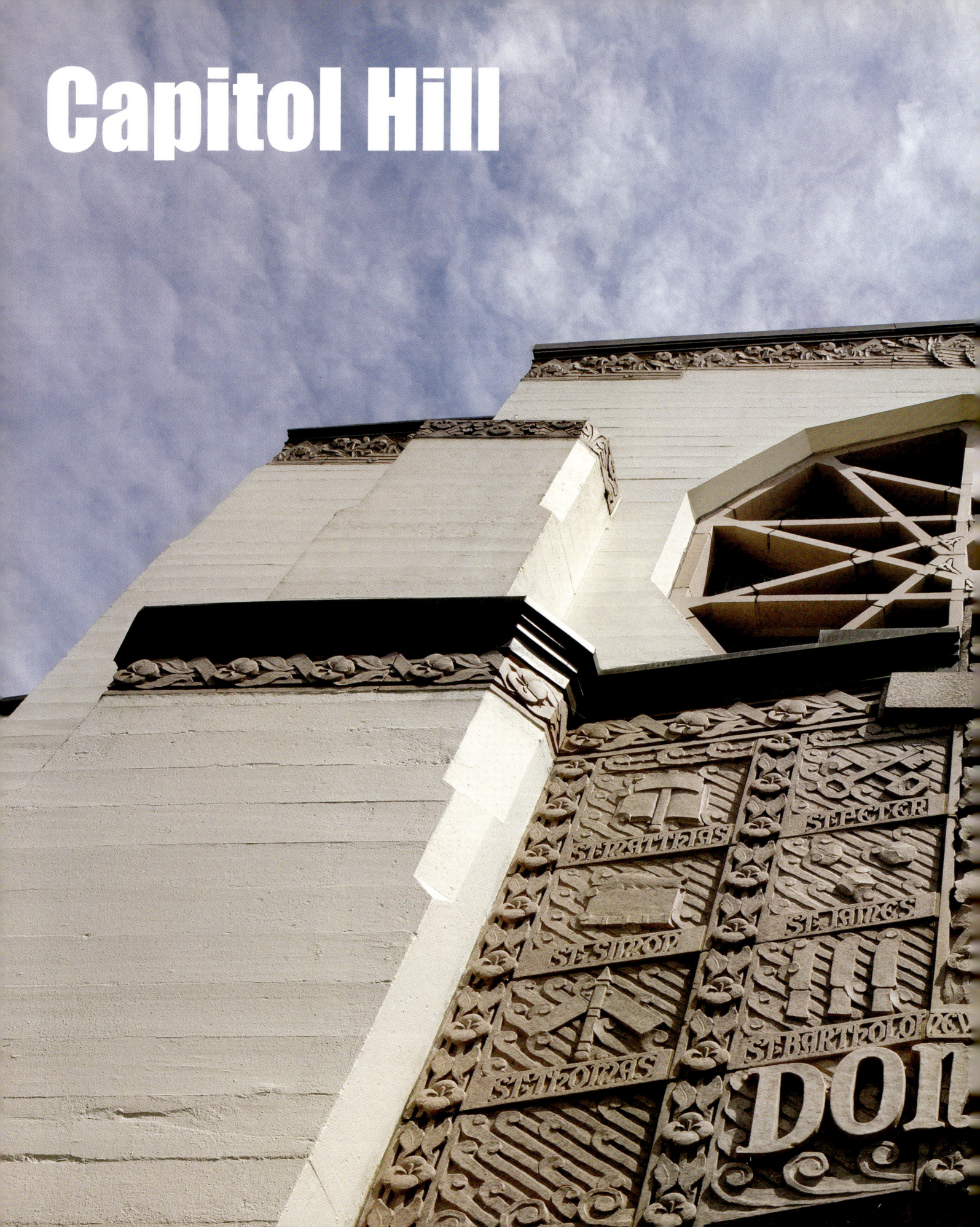
Capitol Hill

St. Joseph

Epiphany of Seattle

Nestled in the Madrona neighborhood is Epiphany of Seattle, an Episcopal church with over a century of serving as a "neighborhood church for the city of Seattle."

Epiphany was founded in 1907 in the back of a neighborhood grocery store. The church building, on the corner of Denny and 38th Avenue, was completed in 1912, and over the years has expanded to include a rectory, a parish hall, an elementary school (now an independent, nonparochial private school called Epiphany School), a larger sanctuary, and a preschool (an independent, nonparochial school called Epiphany Early Learning Preschool). Over the years Epiphany has sought diversity in its membership, and it was the first Episcopal church in the Diocese of Olympia to ordain a woman.

Epiphany is a place set apart—a spiritual oasis of Christian hospitality, dedicated to supporting people wherever they are on their spiritual journey. Epiphany is a place of gathering and conversation, where belonging takes precedence, and relationship is primary—relationship between individuals and their innate gifts, among people, and between people and God.

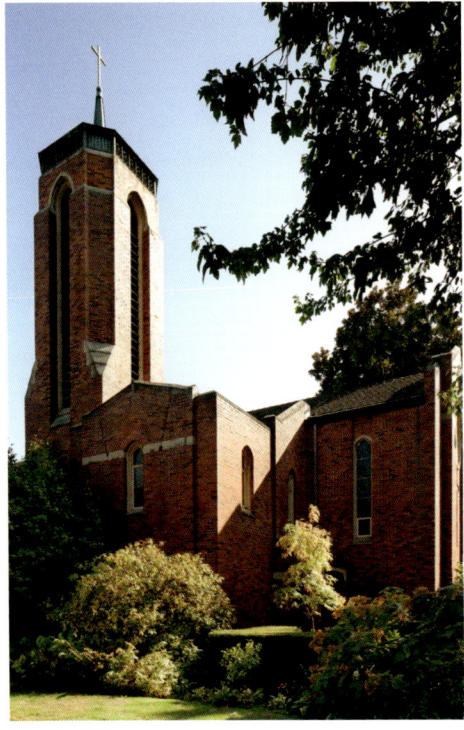

Architecture:
Harold C. Whitehouse, 1950

First A.M.E. Church – Seattle

When discussing which Seattle churches have had the most influence on the history and culture of the city, First African Methodist Episcopal (FAME) would have to be high on anyone's list. Since its beginning as the Jones Street Church at its present location on 14th Avenue on Capitol Hill in 1890, FAME and its leadership have helped define and put in perspective African-American issues and concerns while promoting dialogue among the churches.

The First African Methodist Episcopal denomination began in 1816 in Philadelphia as the first African-American denomination organized in the United States. In 1890 in Seattle, Seaborn J. Collins and laity members transformed the burgeoning Sunday school into an official AMEC organization, purchasing a house that was used until the present church building was erected in 1912. The church expanded when Puget Sound's African-American population grew during World War II, which put FAME in a prime position to effect discussion around civil rights policies surfacing in the 1950s and '60s in Seattle.

Beyond the broad specific social issues, FAME and its leadership have had a great spriritual influence on its parishioners, at last count nearly 2,000 strong. The A.M.E. emphasis on "self-help, self-esteem, and spiritual integrity" is incorporated in the programs and outreach of the church, which includes a sister church (FAME South) in Kent.

Architecture:
Unknown, 1912
Benjamin F. McAdoo, 1955

Greek Orthodox Church of the Assumption

A mission statement can speak volumes. For the Greek Orthodox Church of the Assumption on Capitol Hill, that includes "growing in communion with Jesus Christ our God in worship and sacramental participation, keeping our children with God by love and spiritual instruction, and bringing all to Orthodox Christianity through active worship and holy witness."

Since Greeks started settling in Seattle in the 1870s, many have searched for communities of faith, and the Greek Orthodox Church of the Assumption has been one ministry that has reached out to them and others interested in the Orthodox faith. To expand their outreach recently, the church completed a 15,000-square-foot addition to their existing church building that includes classrooms, meeting spaces, a social hall, and a beautiful skylight atrium.

The church is a member of the Greek Orthodox Archdiocese of America; its "Studies in the Faith" program offers a foundational understanding of the Orthodox Christian faith. Other programs include a dance ministry, a church bookstore, and a Y2A Youth and Young Adult Ministry.

Architecture:
Don McKee, 1961
Demetriou Architects, 2012

Holy Names Academy Chapel

Overlooking the east side of Capitol Hill is Holy Names Academy, an all-girls Catholic high school whose majestic dome and neoclassical architecture are a local and civic treasure. On the third floor, north side of the building is the school chapel, a place for student worship and reflection as well as a beautiful setting for many Catholic weddings.

The school was founded in downtown Seattle in 1880 by the Sisters of the Holy Names of Jesus and Mary, and the present edifice was dedicated in 1908. When the chapel was being added in 1925, special attention was focused on its elegant oak pews and floors, features that remain today. Soon after the chapel was established, marble altars and a pipe organ were added, and in 1939 Sister Editha and her art students painted the distinctive scrollwork on the sanctuary wall behind the main altar.

This quaint and beautiful chapel is considered the spiritual center of Holy Names, which is the oldest continually operating school in Washington.

Architecture:
Albert Breitung, 1908

St. Demetrios Greek Orthodox Church

An integral part of the Montlake neighborhood is St. Demetrios Greek Orthodox Church, which was designed by Paul Thiry, one of the principal architects of the Seattle World's Fair. The Orthodox faith it embraces emphasizes not only the precepts of the Bible but also a rich church tradition handed down over the centuries.

The history of this fascinating church goes back to the late 1800s, when it was known as the Greek-Russian Church. By 1916 the Greeks wanted their own community and church, and built on the site of the current REI store (off the I-5 freeway). The current St. Demetrios in Montlake was dedicated in March of 1963. For more details on the church's history, please refer to the book *A History of Saint Demetrios Greek Orthodox Church and Her People*.

St. Demetrios is home to nearly 700 families, many of whom are third- and fourth-generation descendants of the founding families of the church. Along with other programs, St. Demetrios hosts several Greek cultural activities and events, including "A Taste of Greece," its annual festival of authentic Greek cooking.

Architecture:
Paul Thiry, 1963

St. Joseph

A bedrock institution of Capitol Hill is St. Joseph, a Roman Catholic church and parish that in 2007 celebrated its 100th birthday at its present location on the corner of 18th Avenue East and East Aloha Street. The parish now includes over 1,200 households and has been a center of life for thousands of parishioners, generation after generation who grew up on "Catholic Hill" and reaped the benefits of St. Joseph's ministry and education (a grammar school is part of the parish).

The first church building was dedicated on the site in 1907, a small wood-framed edifice attended mostly by second-generation Irish working-class immigrants. The church grew steadily over the years, and in 1930 the present church—housing over 1,000—was built. An art deco design proposed by architect A. H. Albertson overrode the desire of some to go Gothic. A. H.'s design has stood the test of time, as St. Joseph is now designated a historical landmark.

The church has a strong commitment to social justice issues, supporting the Jubilee Women's Center, transitional housing for women, and St. Martin de Porres homeless shelter downtown, among other outreaches. The continuing legacy of St. Joseph is thus both to the neighborhood and to the city.

Architecture:
A. H. Albertson, 1930

Saint Mark's Cathedral

From its perch on Capitol Hill overlooking the city and above the I-5 freeway, Saint Mark's Episcopal Cathedral is a Seattle institution, well known for its architecture and multifaceted outreach. Saint Mark's is not only a parish church but also the Cathedral church for the Diocese of Olympia, the Episcopal Church in Western Washington, and the seat of its Bishop.

Saint Mark's has a colorful history, dating back to its beginnings in 1889 as a "less formal" worship option to Trinity Church, Seattle's oldest Episcopal parish (established in 1865). The church bought land to build a "Victory Cathedral" at its present site in 1923, opening its doors in 1931. As funds decreased during the Depression, not only were less ambitious plans implemented, but a for-sale sign was placed on the front lawn (making national news) in 1941. The church has been through several remodels and extensions and added buildings over the past 65 years.

Saint Mark's features extensive programming for children and adults and practices "radical hospitality," not only within their own community, but also to the homeless and powerless throughout the city. And if you're looking for a deeply moving experience of worship and meditation, treat yourself to Saint Mark's Compline, an ancient service that has been sung every Sunday evening at the church for more than 50 years.

Architecture:
Arthur Brown Jr. & E. Frere Champney Architects, 1928
Cardwell/Thomas & Associates, 1991
Olson Sundberg, 1997

"What God does first and best and most is to trust his people with their moment in history."

Walter Brueggemann

St. Patrick

With an active, intimate community of around 250 households drawn from all over greater Seattle, St. Patrick is a dynamic Roman Catholic church with a rich history of progressive outreach and creative ministries. And it has shamrocks on its administration building! This is a church that knows how to do justice to its Irish namesake and gets some fun exposure in its neighborhood.

St. Patrick's parish was founded in 1918 under Irish-born pastor Father Michael O'Dwyer, and a combined church and school building was constructed five years later. All went rather swimmingly until 1959, when the planned construction of Interstate 5 cut a swath through the heart of St. Patrick and the homes of about 200 parishioners. After a few back-and-forths with the City Council, the church was given a new site at its present location on Broadway East, with the new building featuring a 65,000-piece Venetian tile mosaic of St. Patrick above the entrance.

In terms of ministry, the church boasts extensive peace and justice efforts, a desire for ecumenical and interfaith dialogue, and innovative liturgies. The 10:00 a.m. Sunday Mass is interpreted for deaf/blind parishioners coming from throughout the Greater Seattle area.

And God knows what they do on St. Patrick's Day.

Architecture:
Ralph Lund, 1961

Saint Nicholas Russian Orthodox Cathedral

With its exquisite architecture showcasing four distinctive onion domes, Saint Nicholas Russian Orthodox Cathedral is a city landmark in Seattle. Working in conjunction with the church, the Saint Nicholas Foundation not only helps to preserve this beautiful church but also works to serve the local community.

The church had its inception in 1932, with a base of membership formed from a group of emigrants who fled Russia during the revolution and some people displaced by the Japanese occupation of Manchuria. Several of the current church members are second- and third-generation descendants of these original members.

Services are held on Saturday evenings and Sunday mornings; visitors often enjoy the a cappella singing of the choir. The church hosts an annual Russian food bazaar with stalls serving traditional Russian food and a vodka-tasting bar!

Architecture:
Ivan Palmaw, 1937

University Christian Church

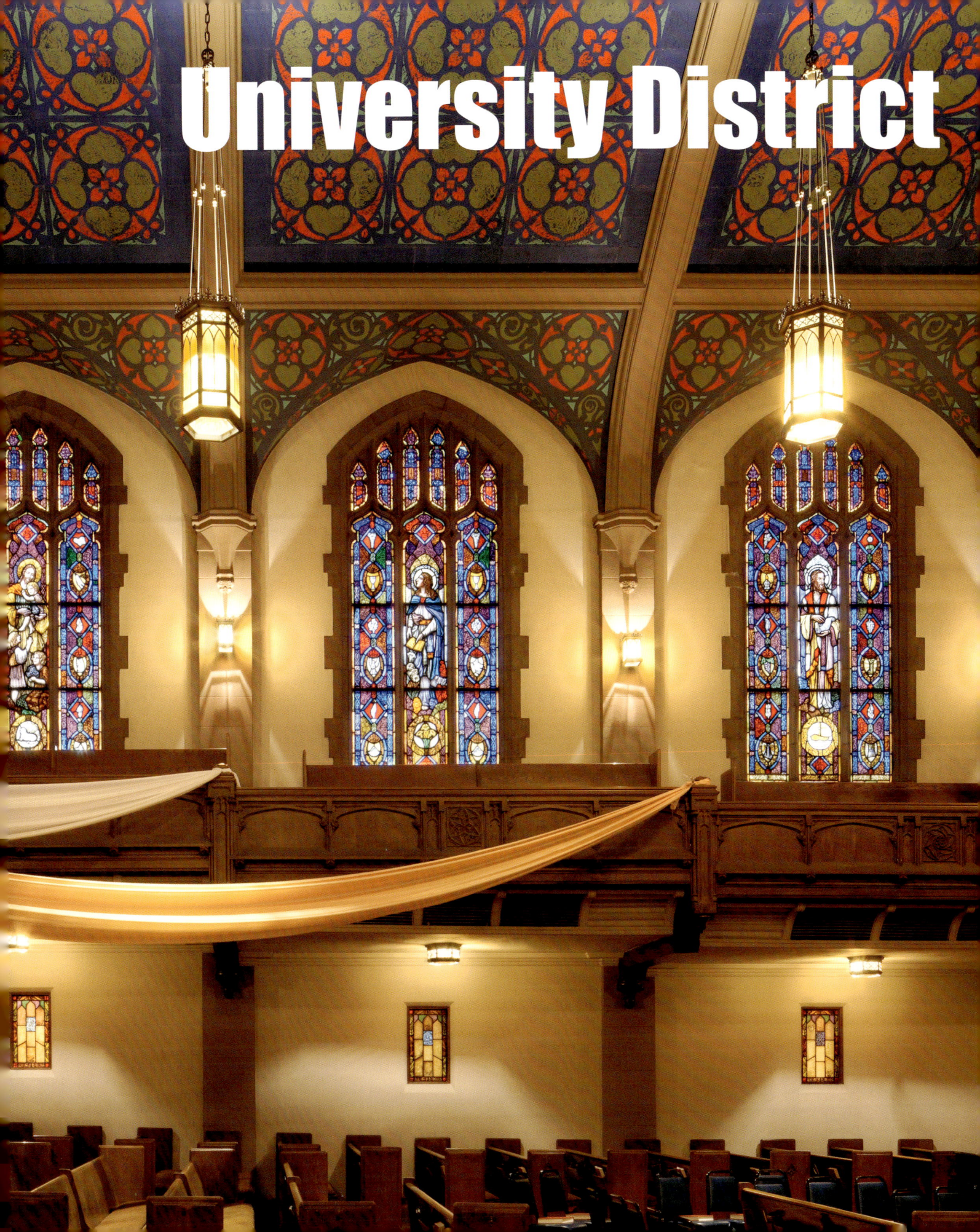

University District

Blessed Sacrament Church

An influential landmark of the University District, Blessed Sacrament is a Dominican parish of the Roman Catholic Church. With a mission "to praise, to bless, to preach," Blessed Sacrament boasts not only breathtaking architecture but also a legacy of over a hundred years of outreach and ministry throughout the city.

The English Gothic masterpiece we see today on 9th Avenue NE was several years in the making, as the coming of World War I and budget constraints pushed the intended completion date from 1910 to 1925. The finished product was worth the wait. The building has since gone through three renovations, one of which was undertaken in 1958 for the parish's 50th anniversary. On February 28, 2001 (ironically, Ash Wednesday), the Nisqually Earthquake damaged the church, and the past decade has been spent not only fixing and retrofitting but also restoring the splendor of the building.

The Dominicans (Order of Preachers) was started in France in 1216 by St. Dominic and has continued to be influential in both the United States and throughout the world. As a Dominican parish, Blessed Sacrament emphasizes prayer and study along with an outreach program that includes a Peace and Justice Committee and a "hospital and homebound" ministry.

Architecture:
Beezer Brothers, 1925

"You can safely assume that you've created God in your own image when it turns out that God hates all the same people you do."

Anne Lamott

University Christian Church

As a "progressive witness" to Seattle since 1890 and to the University District since the beginning of the 20th century, University Christian Church features not only a rich history but also a diverse membership that prides itself on being an open and affirming congregation.

When the University of Washington moved to its present location in 1895 after years downtown, churches began to open up outreaches to the students in the new area, and University Christian was one of the first. Over the years their ministry to questioning students in an academic environment has continued to inform their various programs and outreaches.

Among the present worship opportunities UCC offers are a traditional worship, an early worship, and a Lectio Divina, a practice of Scripture reading, meditation, and prayer. The church also showcases adult forums, a Christian Women's Fellowship (CWF), and a Children's Education department. UCC is affiliated with the Christian Church (Disciples of Christ) denomination.

Architecture:
Clare Moffitt, 1928

University Congregational Church

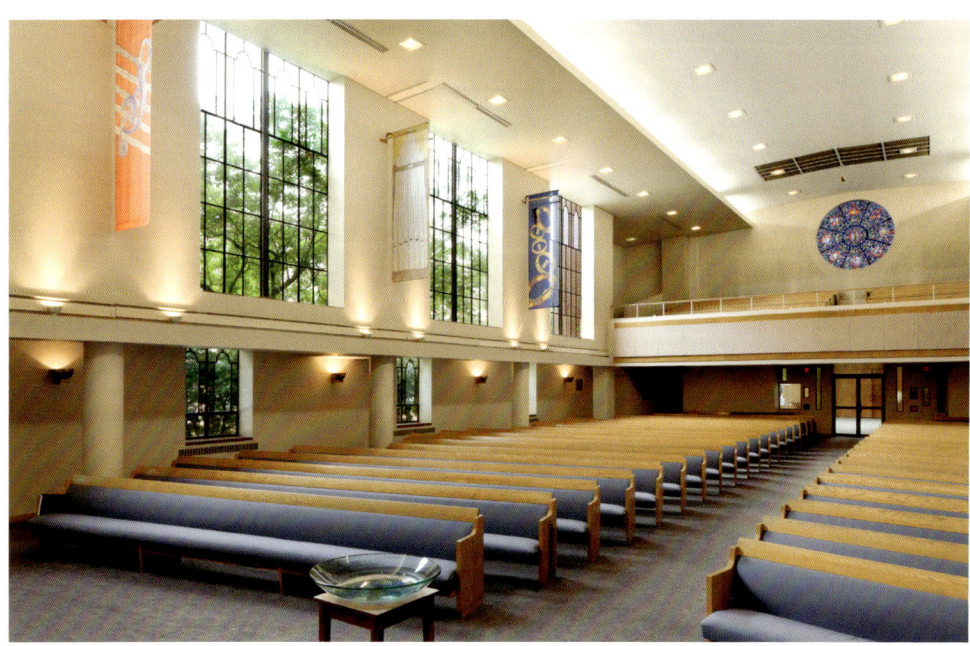

"You are welcome . . . whether you are a believer, a seeker, or a doubter." This statement encapsulates the ministerial perspective of University Congregational Church, an inclusive, progressive Protestant church that has exerted a pivotal influence on the University District for more than 100 years.

Established in 1891 as the first church in the newly forming U District, UCC moved to their current site at the northwest corner of campus in 1953. The church became known for its progressive and stimulating preaching; Dale Turner (who served from 1958 to 1982 as the church's senior minister) was especially well known locally and nationally as an excellent speaker.

Worship at UCC features both traditional and contemporary forms and is backed by a 70-plus-voice choir. Opportunities for contemplation include a weekly "Inviting Silence" meditation time and Taizé Services each Wednesday.

Architecture:
John Paul Jones and
   Leonard Bindon, 1953
TRA Architects, 1989

University Presbyterian Church

"Alive in Jesus, alive together, living for the world." With this core experience, University Presbyterian Church and its thousands of members have been an indispensable community of outreach to the University District for more than a century.

Built two blocks from the University of Washington in the early 20th century after the campus had moved from downtown, University Presbyterian has always put great emphasis on campus ministry. Every Tuesday for several decades the church has offered The Inn, a large worship service attended by students and their friends. UPres is a member of the Presbyterian Church (USA), the biggest Presbyterian denomination in the United States.

Beyond the campus and University District, UPC supports over 30 missionaries and ministry partners in the United States and abroad, and sends hundreds of its members on short-term international missions. Locally the church partners with more than a dozen urban ministries, including Urban Impact, the University District Food Bank, Street Youth Ministries, and Side-by-Side, which supports families who have children with cancer.

Architecture:
Whitehouse and Price, 1951

University Unitarian Church

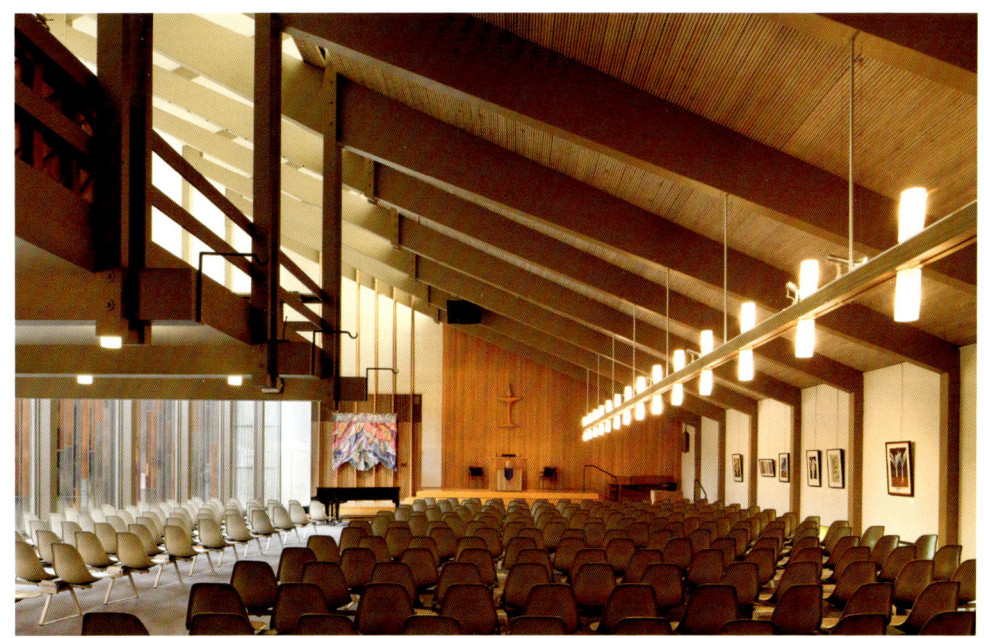

Celebrating its 100th anniversary of ministry this year to the University area and beyond, University Unitarian Church has a long legacy of social justice ministry and open-mindedness to the religious questions of the day.

Throughout the years UUC has partnered with and established several social justice ministries and has made outreach a cornerstone of the church. Currently UUC is active in immigration and campaign finance reforms, transitional housing, and equal rights legislation.

UUC is a Unitarian Universalist church (the separate streams of Unitarianism and Universalism joined together in 1961), a "non-creedal" faith that has its roots in both the Christian and Jewish traditions. Unitarian Universalism has more than a thousand churches in the United States and Canada.

Architecture:
Paul Hayden Kirk, 1959

Seattle Vineyard

On the corner of Brooklyn Avenue NE and 42nd in the University District lies the Seattle Vineyard, a church featuring contemporary worship and a "radical inclusiveness" based on Christ's call to spread the good news. They comically deem their personal style "World Beat Victorian Hippie." On any given Sunday, the congregation might host a mix of neighborhood youth or a group of globetrotters from anywhere in the world.

The Seattle Vineyard had its start in 1987 and moved into this building in 1991. It is part of the Vineyard Movement, one rooted in charismatic renewal, which started in 1975 in Southern California. In 2006, the congregation began the task of renovating the building to reflect its historical architectural style as well as the congregation's roots in mid-1970s West Coast Christianity.

A casual Sunday service starts at 10:00 and features both worship and praise, usually concluding with open communion. Included in the church's ministries are an arts program and what is called Ave-Related Ministries, a discussion group about Christ with street-involved youth.

Architecture:
George Wesley Bullard, 1907

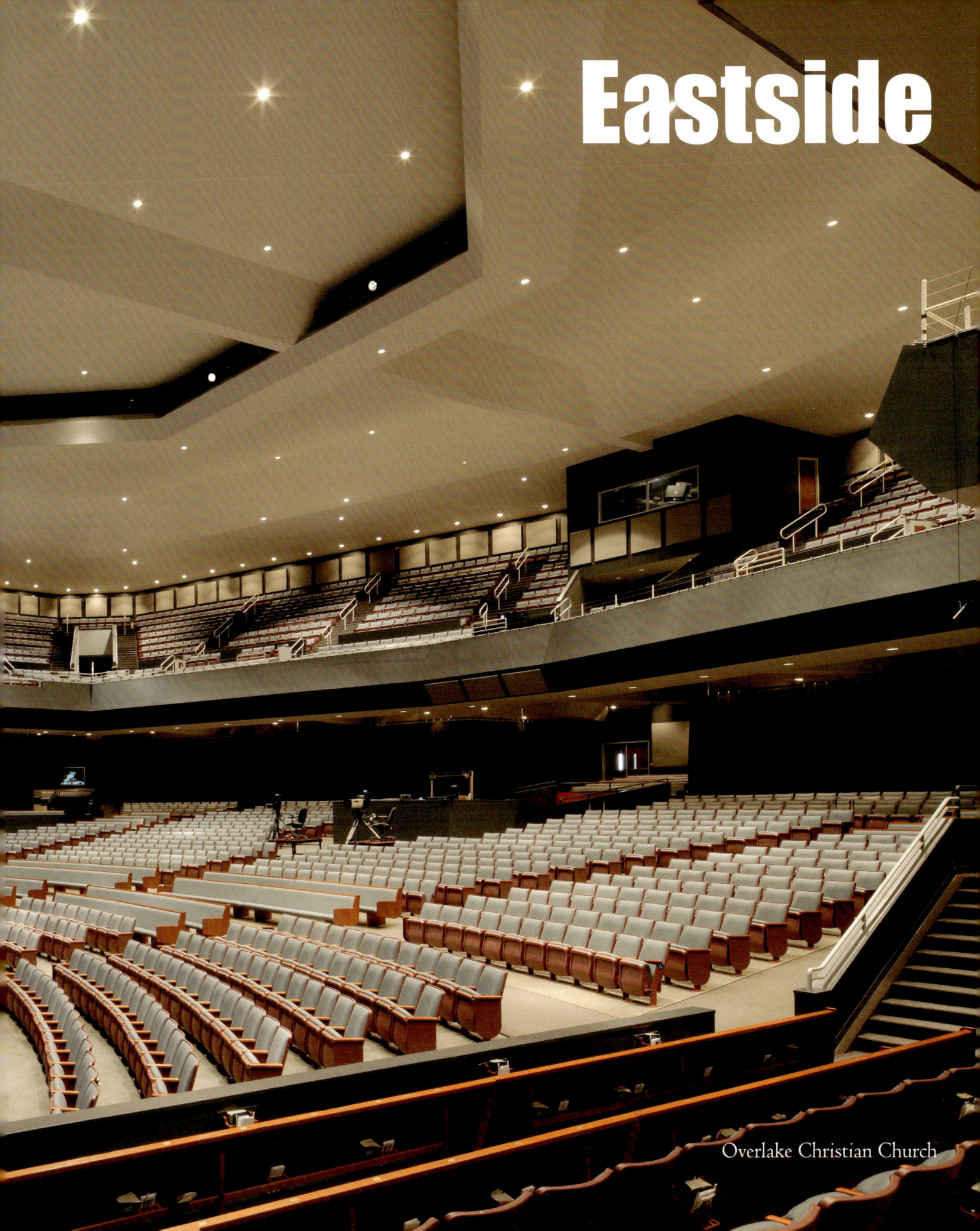

Eastside

Overlake Christian Church

Bellevue Presbyterian Church

One of the largest and most influential churches on the Eastside is Bellevue Presbyterian, which offers a wide variety of opportunities for spiritual growth and outreach to the community.

BelPres has ministries for all ages along with music and adult education programs, Bible studies, and both global and local mission trips. Community outreach includes tutoring and mentoring at-risk children and partnering with local schools to help out in various ways. Their highest desire is to participate with Jesus to revive the Eastside and beyond.

Bellevue Pres is a member of Presbyterian Church USA and is affiliated with the Fellowship of Presbyterians, a new organization developed by BelPres and other churches with similar theology and mission.

Architecture:
Mithun Partners, 2009

Christ Church Kirkland

One of the most vibrant and creative churches on the Eastside is Christ Church Kirkland, which began as a home group ministry in 1972 and has since blossomed into a church with a thousand in attendance.

The ministry begat in the early seventies began birthing other ministries until 1985, when the leadership felt called to begin a church on the Eastside, first meeting at Carl Sandburg Elementary School. In 1991 the ministry bought the Spectra Lux office building and converted it into a church, completely remodeling the building in 2003.

The church features many creative ministries, including a discipleship program called the Master's Commission and a School of Prophetic Arts. It also has the unique Christ Church Kirkland Cooperative School, which combines a home-school emphasis on parental teaching with the benefits of meeting together in the church facility.

Architecture:
Baylis Architects, 2003

Eastridge Church

Eastridge Church is a vibrant and growing Eastside congregation built upon contemporary worship and a strong emphasis on relevant Bible teaching. Their variety of ministries are based on building lives for God in a fun and exciting atmosphere, and have outreach to the entire family.

Eastridge's mission statement centers on three key principles:

- To be an Outreach church – Reaching out to the community and the I-90 corridor and to the ends of the earth with the life-giving message of Jesus Christ.
- To be an Embracing church – that embraces people of all walks of life.
- To be a Discipling church – Building an infrastructure of discipleship so that each age bracket can experience and grow in the fullness of Christ.

Eastridge stands out as one of the most vibrant churches on the Eastside. Their new campus features outstanding craftsmanship, state-of-the-art theatrical design in the sanctuary, a dynamic children's ministry area, a preschool for ages 2 through 5, a Learning Center that offers all-day childcare, a full commercial kitchen, a full-service café, and a separate Student Center.

Mars Hill Church Bellevue

In the heart of downtown Bellevue lies Mars Hill Church Bellevue, opened in 2011 in the former John Danz Theatre, and currently the largest Mars Hill location.

Mars Hill Church began in 1996 as a Bible study in the living room of WSU graduate Mark Driscoll and his wife, Grace. Mars Hill currently has 14 locations in four states (Washington, Oregon, California, and New Mexico) and was named the third fastest growing and second most innovative church in America by *Outreach* Magazine. The John Danz Theatre features classic sixties architecture and is named for an early Seattle film exhibitor who owned a thriving movie-house business and opened the theatre on December 22, 1961, featuring Elvis Presley in *Blue Hawaii*.

Mars Hill Bellevue offers three services every Sunday and features Bible-preaching, kids' programs, and original music with fresh takes on older hymns. The church often hosts conferences and seminars, as well as weekly Community Groups in neighborhoods throughout the Eastside. Mars Hill also supports local organizations including Jubilee Reach and Seattle's Union Gospel Mission.

"The point of having an open mind, like an open mouth, is to close it on something solid."

G. K. Chesterton

Mary Queen of Peace

A thriving Roman Catholic parish on the Sammamish Plateau, Mary Queen of Peace is home to more than 2,100 families. With unique architecture (tongue-in-cheekly described as the "holy spaceship" or "launching pad to heaven") and creative outreach, MQP is a testimony to how a contemporary church can become a vital community.

The parish was founded in 1987 by the Archdiocese in response to the population growth in the Sammamish area. The church was dedicated in 1990, and a few years later the Parish Center was in place; in recent years came the completion of a new tabernacle in the chapel and the Resurrection Garden.

The church offers a plethora of growth and outreach programs and hosts several social events (dinners, seminars, concerts) where the local community is invited. Further ministry includes a Helping Hands Meal Ministry and a Human Concerns Commission, which donates to local, national, and international charities. The church also has a sister parish relationship with Our Lady of the Annunciation in Tamale, Ghana.

Architecture:
Becker Architects, 1989

Mercer Island Presbyterian Church

A thriving church community on the Eastside, Mercer Island Presbyterian Church (MIPC) is an open and affirming congregation with a commitment to "seeking God, sharing our gifts, and serving others."

The present-day facility had its origins in 1963, when famous architect Paul Thiry completed a hexagonal sanctuary seating 350 people, which has since been renovated and expanded. Corporate worship is central to the life of MIPC, with weekly Sunday offerings including a breakfast service, a traditional service, and a more contemporary evening service.

Serving as a partner and resource to the local community is also vital to MIPC. They have a long-standing tradition of vibrant and diverse opportunities for children, youth, adults, and families. In the early 1990s, the church established its own Foundation, with the express goal of having 100% of its disbursements used for service and mission. A variety of partnerships and opportunities are devoted to serving the poor, working for justice, and sharing God's love primarily through health, education, and housing.

Architecture:
Paul Thiry, 1963
Broweleit Peterson Hammer
    Architects, 2001

Overlake Christian Church

One of the largest and most well-known churches on the Eastside is Overlake Christian Church, a nondenominational congregation in Redmond that states, "No perfect people allowed."

The church began in Kirkland in 1968 and grew from a ministry of 27 people to more than 6,000. In 1997 the church moved from Kirkland to a new 250,000-square-foot facility on 27 acres in Redmond.

The church offers a plethora of possibilities for service and outreach, including life groups, caring and student ministries, short-term international missions teams, and support groups like Celebrate Recovery (a 12-step program based on Jesus' teachings). Over the years, Overlake has started eight other churches throughout the Puget Sound region.

Architecture:
Acts, LLC, 1997

Queen Anne

Queen Anne Lutheran

Bethany Presbyterian Church

On the top of Queen Anne Hill you'll find Bethany Presbyterian Church, a creative and thriving Presbyterian Church USA congregation of about 600 people that puts an emphasis on outreach ministry, with more than 20% of the church budget being spent outside the church.

Bethany had its start in the 1880s as Second Presbyterian Church, which was created to minister to "North Seattle," or Belltown. The name was changed to Bethany ("home of the friends of Jesus") in 1903, and the church moved to a second location at 1st Avenue North and Roy Street in 1907. Its current building at the top of Queen Anne was erected in 1930.

The outreach ministry features their Wednesday Night Dinners program, which brings together the congregation, the homeless, and the wider community. The church also has an extensive Arts Ministry that encompasses the visual arts, performance, sculpture, and music and encourages people of all ages to become involved.

Architecture:
James Hay, 1929

First Free Methodist Church

Located on the north end of Queen Anne Hill across from Seattle Pacific University, First Free Methodist Church has several compelling ministries and a rich history of over 130 years of outreach in the Seattle area.

First Free Methodist started as a "downtown" church in 1880, being the eighth church organized in the city. In 1906, the church became associated with Seattle Seminary (now Seattle Pacific University) and became the Second Free Methodist Church, but regained its original status of "First" in 1924. The current brick structure located at 3rd Avenue West and West Dravus Street was built in 1956, with the attractive Fine Center built in 1994.

The Free Methodist denomination was founded before the Civil War, with the "free" signifying no restrictions for women, blacks, the poor, or new immigrants flocking into the country. In keeping with that history, FFMC generously supports 17 Seattle-based agencies as a part of its Local Outreach program, including Puget Sound Christian Clinic, Operation Nightwatch, and the Union Gospel Mission.

Architecture:
Durham, Anderson and Freed, 1994

Queen Anne Baptist Church

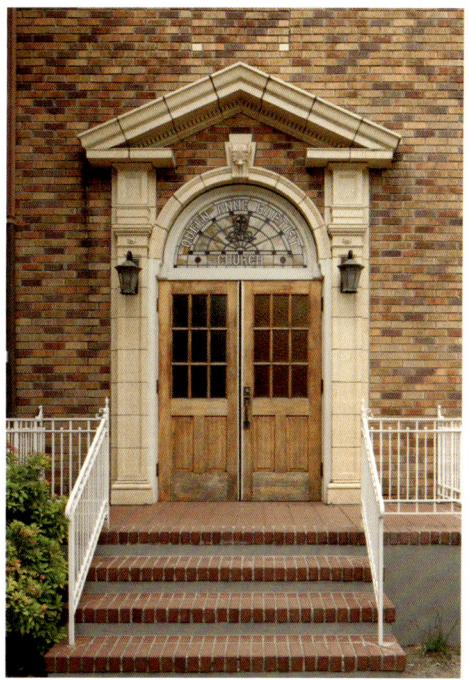

Overlooking the summit of Queen Anne Hill, Queen Anne Baptist Church has a rich history and dynamic outreach.

Queen Anne Baptist was established in 1886, building its first church at the current location in 1926. The building was enlarged in 1936 and 1957. The church is affiliated with American Baptist Churches USA, a denomination with over 5,200 local congregations across the United States and Puerto Rico.

Queen Anne Baptist houses two preschools—a co-op preschool and the Sweet Pea Cottage Preschool for the Arts. The church supports various outreach projects, including Queen Anne Helpline, the Mary Magdalene Shelter for Homeless Women, and Children's Dance Workshop.

Architecture:
Frederick V. Lockman and
   G. E. Merrill, 1936

Queen Anne Lutheran Church

Queen Anne Lutheran Church is located at the top of Queen Anne Hill. Its stated mission is "proclaiming God's love in Christ for every person."

Members are offered several ministry opportunities during the week, including an Adult Forum each Sunday to discuss Christian issues, a Brown Bag Bible Study each Tuesday, and a Faith and Film group that talks about popular movies each month. Outreach at QALC includes Project HomeBase, a program that helps the homeless shelter Mary's Place.

In 2010 the church celebrated its 90-year history of excellence in worship and music by installing a new world-class pipe organ. The church is a member of the Evangelical Lutheran Church in America.

Architecture:
Durham, Anderson and Freed, 1959
Broderick Architects, 2008

Sacred Heart of Jesus

At the bottom of Queen Anne Hill stands the Catholic Parish Sacred Heart of Jesus, a welcoming community and nurturing presence in this area for more than 120 years.

Redemptorist priests and brothers, their religious congregation founded in 1732 by St. Alphonsus Liguori, have been serving here since June of 1891, with an emphasis on spreading the Good News of Jesus Christ and reaching out to the poor and most abandoned. Key ministries today are sheltering the needy and homeless, the Queen Anne Food Bank at Sacred Heart with hot meals and food assistance, and daily opportunities for the Sacraments of Reconciliation and the Eucharist.

A thriving Young Adult Ministry, Seniors Group, and Legion of Mary reach out to the homebound and marginalized in a variety of ways. Lay ministers are integral to the community and enable ever-growing opportunities for outreach. The spirit is embracing, caring, generous, and service oriented.

Architecture:
Paul Thiry, 1960

St. Paul's Episcopal Church

Poised at the bottom of Queen Anne Hill and fitting its billing as "a spiritual oasis in the city," St. Paul's Episcopal Church features a distinctive design, a firm commitment to the arts, and a liturgy that expresses both the beauty and profundity of God.

With its music, drama, painting, sculpture, and poetry, St. Paul's communicates its belief in the synthesis between the arts, religion, and spirituality. In addition to the many artists who are members, the church has an artist-in-residence program in which local artists offer their work within the liturgy.

The church has gone through a recent renovation, using natural, native materials to augment the building's aesthetic and add to its beauty. The addition of a full-immersion baptismal font harmonizes with other creative aspects of the church, including its "suspended" organ, creatively carved crucifix, and icons.

Architecture:
Steinhart, Theriault & Anderson Architects, 1962
atelierjones, 2012

"God does not want us to do extraordinary things; He wants us to do ordinary things extraordinarily well."

Bishop Charles Gore

Seattle Church of Christ

Featuring a dynamic outreach and showcasing breathtaking architecture from a building with landmark status, Seattle Church of Christ on Queen Anne Hill is a congregation "committed to celebrating the work of God in our lives, and becoming a light to those around us."

The building was erected in 1926 and for many years was the Seventh Church of Christ Scientist before becoming Seattle Church of Christ in 2008. Many local organizations use the building, including the Queen Anne Historical Society and the local Queen Anne Girl Scout Troop, and the church is popular as a location for weddings.

Seattle Church of Christ showcases several ministries, including an outreach to students at the University of Washington and Seattle Pacific, a Chemical Recovery program, and an involvement with HOPE worldwide–Washington, where the members have unique opportunities to serve the poor and needy both in Washington State and around the world. Seattle Church of Christ is a member of the International Churches of Christ and also holds an Eastside service.

Architecture:
Harlan Thomas, 1926

Southwest

Fauntleroy Church

Fauntleroy Church – United Church of Christ

Beside Fauntleroy Creek in the West Seattle community of Fauntleroy stands Fauntleroy Church, a historic and progressive neighborhood church that proclaims, "Whoever you are and wherever you are on life's journey, you are welcome here."

The church had its origin in 1908, when a small group of members constructed "The Church that was built in a day" in the sparsely settled Fauntleroy area. Steady church growth over the next several decades led to the construction of a new facility in the 1950s, featuring its soon-to-be-famous window wall, bringing the outdoors into the sanctuary.

The community of Fauntleroy Church offers a myriad of ways to get involved, including social, ministry, and action groups. Their outreach programs are comprised of several task forces, including the Green Committee, Homelessness Task Force, Global Peace and Justice Task Force, and Oaxaca Mission Project.

Architecture:
Robert Durham, 1951

Holy Rosary

A beautiful church in the West Seattle area, Holy Rosary Catholic Church is an outreach that refers to itself as The House of God (Domus Dei) and The House of the People (Domus Ecclesiae) and has a rich history of ministry to the surrounding neighborhood.

Holy Rosary Parish began in 1909, when 35 families got together in the West Seattle community called the Admiral District. In 1937, ground was broken for the present Tuscan Romanesque-style church, which was completed and dedicated that year. In 1997 a fire caused extensive smoke damage and some structural damage to the church; after months of reconstruction and renovation, the church reopened in 1998.

Holy Rosary calls itself "A Stewardship Parish" and its many service ministries include a soup kitchen, a women's shelter, a Green Team, and a social justice ministry. The parish also houses Holy Rosary School, which goes from prekindergarten through eighth grade.

Architecture:
Father James F. Lanigan, 1937

Japanese Baptist Church

Organized in 1899, the exquisite Japanese Baptist Church of Seattle has a long history of dynamic ministry to both the Japanese community and the local neighborhood. In many ways the history of this church and the story of Japanese-Americans in Seattle intertwine.

Soon after its inception, the church began working with the "Fujin Home," an outreach to the large numbers of picture brides who came to Seattle to marry local men sight unseen. With World War II and the forced evacuation of all Japanese-Americans from the West Coast, the church had to close temporarily but ministered to the many displaced in the area. Throughout its more than 110 years of existence, the church has maintained strong ties to the local Japanese-American community and culture.

Along with its beautiful sanctuary, the church showcases a Japanese Garden at the side of the building. It has an excellent Christian Education program for English- and Japanese-speaking people and a history of generous giving to missions.

Architecture:
Milton Stricker, 1985

Our Lady of Mount Virgin

In the Mount Baker neighborhood lies Our Lady of Mount Virgin, a Roman Catholic church and parish that started in 1911.

When it was first established, Our Lady of Mount Virgin served as a parish for the Italian immigrant community that had settled in South Seattle. The name Our Lady of Mount Virgin came from Italy; there are many other congregations with the same name across the United States. Recently the church has also included a number of Asian families.

The church ministers to over 400 families and has several classes for its members, including Confirmation and Communion. It offers masses on Sunday at 8:00 a.m. and Tuesday through Friday at 10:00 a.m. Masses with songs in Laotian (9:30 a.m.) and Cantonese and Mandarin (noon) are also offered on Sundays.

Architecture:
Beezer Brothers, 1915

St. Edward

One of the largest and most influential parishes in South Seattle, St. Edward is known for its cultural diversity and ministry to the local neighborhood.

The church and parish were established in 1906, making St. Edward one of the oldest Catholic outreaches in the city of Seattle. The parish is a member of the Archdiocese of Seattle and the Tri-Parish of South Seattle, which includes St. George Parish and St. Paul Parish.

The church offers many resources to its parishioners, including an extensive mass schedule during the week and on weekends, classes, and support for the Society of St. Vincent de Paul. The parish also houses St. Edward School, which offers classes from preschool through eighth grade.

Architecture:
John W. Malone, 1958

"You must live with people to know their problems, and live with God in order to solve them."

Peter Taylor Forsyth

Phinney Ridge Lutheran Church

Northwest

Bethany Community Church

"In essentials, unity; in nonessentials, liberty; in all things, charity." This statement is taken seriously by the leadership and members of Bethany Community Church, a vibrant church in the Green Lake area that opened a new 600-seat sanctuary in 2008.

Bethany began in 1900 as a mission to local Native Americans in the Ballard area and had organized as Bethany Baptist Church by 1916. They stayed in their original building until 1969, when they moved to a newly remodeled building at their present location (North 80th and Stone Avenue North). Since that time, the congregation has grown to over 2,000 people worshipping each Sunday across six different services.

The focus of their outreach program is Tabitha Ministries, launched in 2006, which serves as a hub for Bethany's local ministries. The church also provides extensive discipleship programs for all ages and a full pastoral care program.

Architecture:
Miller Hull Partnership, 2008

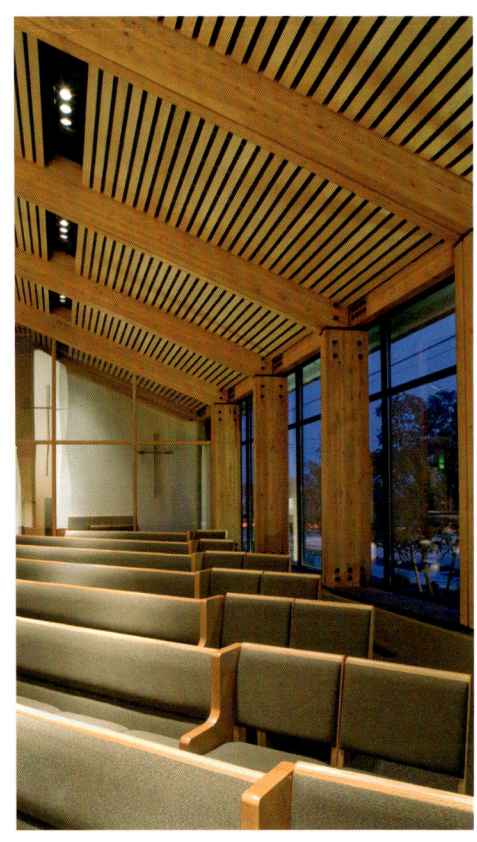

"Churches in cities are most wonderful solitudes."

Thomas Merton

Calvary Christian Assembly

A landmark in Seattle's Roosevelt neighborhood for more than 80 years, Calvary Christian Assembly is a dynamic, intergenerational community with a focus on "helping people find and follow Jesus Christ."

The church was established in 1927 at the southwest corner of 8th Avenue NE and 69th Street, originally named Hollywood Temple. The church experienced significant growth in the ensuing years, changing its name to Calvary Temple and then Calvary Christian Assembly, where in 2003 they dedicated a renovation of the facilities. Northwest Bible Institute started in the church building in 1934; the school is now called Northwest University and resides in Kirkland.

CCA boasts an extensive outreach, with support of humanitarian programs throughout the world, a strong connection with Bread of Life Mission in Seattle, and ownership of an apartment building dedicated to low-income housing near the church. The church is a member of Assemblies of God USA, who with Assemblies of God organizations around the world make up the world's largest Pentecostal denomination, with over 60 million members and adherents.

Architecture:
J. A. Johnson, 1951

Green Lake United Methodist Church

With a church building now known as "The Castle" for its unique and attractive stone architecture, Green Lake United Methodist is a warm and embracing church community that has been at its present location for over a century.

It was in 1903 that the loving hands of 50 original members worked together to build a small, striking church with stones from Green Lake. Many of these original stones were used to construct the larger stone castle in 1910. Originally founded as Green Lake Methodist Episcopal Church, Green Lake United Methodist remains a cornerstone of the Green Lake community.

Although the stone castle is historic, the ministries of the church reach out into the modern world. Supporting Mary's Place and Angeline's Day Center, organizations that support and lift up homeless women and children, the church engages in works of love and justice. This small congregation with a big heart welcomes people of all ages, including young adults, to ministries that meet in nontraditional locations like a bar for discussions at Pub Theology. The church facility is available for weddings and concerts.

Architecture:
Rich & Trimble Associates, 1910

Interfaith Community Sanctuary

Featuring a historic building and a desire to honor all faith traditions in its worship and community life, Interfaith Community Sanctuary emphasizes a mission to "create a home of love and truth as a center of light for all seekers of divine wisdom."

With a deep connection to the city of Ballard (they share the same birth year), the church was built in 1890 and in 1981 was given landmark designation by the City of Seattle. Several congregations have been housed in this historic building, starting with the German Congregational Church and including the New Age Christian Church (from 1973 to 1998).

Interfaith Community Church was established in 1999. The congregation chose to rename itself Interfaith Community Sanctuary in the fall of 2012. It remains a volunteer organization with no paid staff. The church continues to evolve and grow through its diverse interfaith worship services, public interfaith gatherings, and community service, and regularly collaborates with other faith and spiritual communities in the creation of dialogues, symposiums, and workshops.

Architecture:
Unknown, 1890

Our Lady of Fatima

In the heart of Magnolia is Our Lady of Fatima, a thriving parish of almost 1,200 families that includes a church, a school, and a dynamic ministry to the surrounding area.

The parish began in the early 1950s when St. Margaret's Parish on Queen Anne Hill became overcrowded and Catholics in the Magnolia area needed a home of their own. At first a temporary church was constructed, followed by the splendid present structure; over the years other improvements such as a new Parish Center were built. The church name celebrates the miracles occurring in the town of Fátima in Portugal, where in 1917 the Blessed Virgin Mary appeared to three children.

The church is known for a number of its outreach efforts, including Magnolia Moms, Society of St. Vincent de Paul, and its Music Program. The parish is very proud of its school, which serves nearly 300 students attending in grades K-8.

Architecture:
James Klontz, 1968

Phinney Ridge Lutheran Church

A historic church in North Seattle, Phinney Ridge Lutheran sees its mission as "Opening Doors. Sharing Christ. Serving the World."

The congregation was organized as Bethel Norwegian Lutheran Church in 1915, with a small chapel being erected at 1st Avenue NW and West 74th. During World War II the congregation experienced a surge in membership; a new church structure (which is used presently) was deemed necessary and was completed in 1951.

The church website proclaims: "Whether at worship, through educational programs, packaged in a gift from our food bank, in fellowship, through a concert, conversation or prayer, there is an open invitation for you to participate." The church is a member of the ELCA (Evangelical Lutheran Church in America).

Architecture:
Edward Mahlum, 1951

Acknowledgments

To my lovely wife, Hattie, for everything.

To my precious daughter, Rebecca.

To Reverend Dennis Andersen, pastor and Seattle church expert extraordinaire, for help with the History chapter and church selection.

To eminent Seattle historian Paul Dorpat, for initial help with research and direction.

To all the wonderful church contacts who opened up their inner sanctums; a special shout-out to Bob Sittig of Seattle First Baptist, Larry Brouse of St. James Cathedral, Liz Sloat of Saint Mark's Cathedral, and Father John Whitney of St. Joseph's for support at the start of the project.

To my cohorts and professors at the Seattle University School of Theology and Ministry, for helping me see and key on the Light.

To my fellow church members and staff at Bethany Presbyterian, thanks for being such a wonderful church community.

To the fantastic folks at Documentary Media:
To Barry Provorse for embracing and supporting the project.
To Petyr Beck for his wise guidance and support.

To Paul Langland for his artistic sensibilities and commitment to excellence.

And last but not least to Lara Swimmer, Seattle's best photographer, whose work is a beauty to behold.

Bibliography

Bagley, Clarence. *History of Seattle: From the Earliest Settlement to the Present Time.* Seattle: S. J. Clarke Publishing, 1916.

Buerge, David M., and Junius Rochester. *Roots and Branches: The Religious Heritage of Washington State.* Seattle: Church Council of Greater Seattle, 1988.

Dorpat, Paul. *Seattle Now and Then.* Seattle: Tartu Publications, 1990.

Grubb, Norman. *Modern Viking: The Story of Abraham Vereide, Pioneer in Christian Leadership.* Grand Rapids: Zondervan Publishing House, 1961.

Holl, Steven. *The Chapel of St. Ignatius.* New York: Princeton Architectural Press, 1999.

Killen, Patricia O'Connell, and Mark Silk. *Religion and Public Life in the Pacific Northwest: The None Zone.* Walnut Creek: AltaMira Press, 2004.

Ludwig, Carolyn. *Jewels in Our Crown: Churches of Los Angeles.* Los Angeles: Ludwig Publishing Inc., 2003.

Pearson, Arnold, and Esther Pearson. *Early Churches of Washington State.* Seattle: University of Washington Press, 1980.

Putnam, Robert D., and David E. Campbell. *American Grace: How Religion Divides and Unites Us.* New York: Simon & Schuster, 2010.

Shelley, Bruce L. *Church History in Plain Language.* Nashville: Thomas Nelson, Inc., 2008.

Soden, Dale E. *The Reverend Mark Matthews: An Activist in the Progressive Era.* Seattle: University of Washington Press, 2001.

Spaeth, Barbara H. Stenson. *A Bridge Over Time: The Centennial History of the Church of the Epiphany (Seattle) Parish.* Seattle: Epiphany Parish, 2007.